This journal belongs to:

____

13463831R10061

Made in the USA
Lexington, KY
31 October 2018